Milk

Lola Schaefer

Heinemann LIBRARY

www.heinemann.co.uk/library
Visit our website to find out more information about Heinemann Library books.

To order:
☎ Phone 44 (0) 1865 888066
▤ Send a fax to 44 (0) 1865 314091
💻 Visit the Heinemann Bookshop at www.heinemann.co.uk/library to browse our catalogue and order online.

First published in Great Britain by Heinemann Library, Halley Court, Jordan Hill, Oxford OX2 8EJ, part of Harcourt Education. Heinemann is a registered trademark of Harcourt Education Ltd.

Editorial: Diyan Leake and Kristen Truhlar
Design: Joanna Hinton-Malivoire
Picture research: Melissa Allison
Artwork: Big Top
Production: Duncan Gilbert
Originated by Modern Age
Printed and bound in China by South China Printing Co. Ltd.

ISBN 978 0 431 01521 7
12 11 10 09 08
10 9 8 7 6 5 4 3 2 1

British Library Cataloguing in Publication Data
Schaefer, Lola M., 1950-
    Milk. - (Food groups)
    1. Milk - Juvenile literature 2. Dairy products in human nutrition - Juvenile literature 3. Cookery (Milk) - Juvenile literature
    I. Title
    641.3'7

Acknowledgements
The publishers would like to thank the following for permission to reproduce photographs: © Corbis pp. **6** (Royalty Free), **7** (Macduff Everton), **12** (Jamie Grill); © Harcourt Education Ltd/Tudor Photography pp. **4**, **8**, **11**, **17**, **18**, **20**, **21**, **23**, **25**; © istockphoto.com p. **15** (Christine Balderas); Masterfile pp. **24** (Rolf Bruderer), **28** (Norbert Schäfer); © Photolibrary.com p. **29**; © Photolibrary pp. **9** (Botanica), **10** (Anthony Blake Picture Library), **13** (Anthony Blake Picture Library), **14** (Corbis), **19** (Anthony Blake Picture Library), **22** (Anthony Blake Picture Library), **26** (Foodpix), **27** (Plainpicture); © Punchstock p. **16** (itstockfree).

Cover photograph reproduced with permission © Photolibrary.com (Anthony Blake).

Contents

Some words are shown in bold, **like this**. You can find out what they mean by looking in the glossary.

What are milk and milk foods?

Milk is a white liquid made by some female mammals. People drink milk. Butter, cream, cheese, and yoghurt are some of the foods that are made with milk.

All of these foods are made with milk.

Each colour on this plate is for one of the five food groups.

Milk and milk foods are one of the **food groups**. You need to drink milk or eat some milk foods each day. This will help you have a good **diet**.

Where milk comes from

Farmers raise cows or other animals that make milk. The cows or goats **graze** on grasses and hay. Their bodies change the food they eat into milk.

The **nutrients** that cows eat in the grass go into the milk you drink.

Some farmers milk their cows by hand. Others use milking machines.

Farmers milk the cows or other milk-giving animals. They take the milk to a **dairy**. Machines at the dairy prepare the milk and package it. The milk is then sold in shops.

Using milk in foods

Milk is added to many foods. Milk can be used to make pancakes. It can be added to cakes. It is also used in some soups and sauces.

This girl is adding milk to a cake mixture.

Hot chocolate

Please ask an adult to help you.

- Warm the milk in a saucepan.
- Add the cocoa powder.
- Stir until mixed.
- Pour into mugs.
- Serve and enjoy.

You will need:
- enough milk to fill two mugs
- 4 tablespoons of cocoa powder

A hot chocolate is a treat on a cold day.

What milk and milk foods look like

Most milk foods are white or yellow. Milk is a white liquid. Cream is thicker, but also white. When cream is whipped, it is fluffy. Butter is light yellow.

Whipped cream is a tasty topping for fruit.

Cheese can be eaten by itself or cooked with other foods.

Cheese is made from milk. It can be white, yellow, or orange. Swiss cheese has tiny holes. Most cheese is cut into blocks. Some is shredded.

How milk and milk foods taste

Milk is a smooth drink. It has a **mild** flavour and tastes good with many foods. Cream has more flavour than milk.

Butter is made from cream and is a little oily.

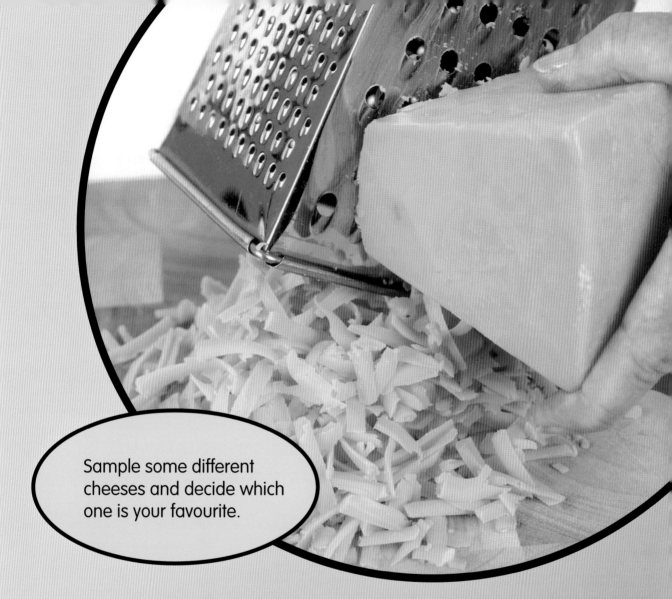

Sample some different cheeses and decide which one is your favourite.

Each cheese has its own flavour. Some are mild. Others are strong and almost **tangy**. Cheddar cheese has a strong taste.

Why milk foods are healthy

Milk and the foods made with milk have a large amount of **calcium**. Calcium is a **mineral** that keeps bones strong. It also helps build strong teeth.

Drink milk and eat milk foods every day to keep your teeth healthy and strong.

Milk is a tasty way to get many **nutrients**.

Milk and milk foods also have **protein**. Protein helps build new bone, skin, muscle, and other parts of the body. These foods also have **vitamin** D that helps keep bones strong.

How many milk foods do you need?

Most children 5–10 years old need 2–3 servings of milk foods each day. Try to eat one serving of milk foods at each of your meals. A serving could be a glass of milk.

Semi-skimmed and skimmed milk have less fat than whole milk.

This lunch has two servings of milk foods.

Another serving of milk food is two slices of cheese. A bowl of yoghurt is a healthy serving of milk food. A small bowl of ice cream is a serving of milk food. Ice cream has a lot of **fat** in it, so you should only eat it as a treat.

Milk foods to eat for breakfast

For breakfast you might drink a glass of milk. Or you might melt cheese in scrambled eggs. Milk on whole grain cereal is a healthy breakfast food.

Many people eat bagels with cream cheese for breakfast.

Fruity yoghurt

Please ask an adult to help you.

- In a tall glass, put a layer of yoghurt.
- Add a layer of berries.
- Now add another layer of yoghurt.
- Repeat another two times.
- Serve and enjoy.

You will need:
- low-**fat** natural yoghurt
- mixed berries, such as strawberries, blackberries, blueberries, or any other that you enjoy eating

This breakfast has milk and fruit, two of the **food groups**.

Milk foods to eat for lunch

A bowl of creamed soup makes a tasty lunch. Milk or cream is in these soups. Cheese pizza is a good lunch.

Try eating cottage cheese and fruit on top of crackers.

Buttery vegetables

Please ask an adult to help you.

- Melt the butter in a frying pan over a medium heat.
- Add the vegetables and cook until tender.
- Add salt and pepper to taste.
- Serve and enjoy.

For each person, you will need:
- 3 tablespoons (tbsp) vegetables cut into bite-sized pieces
- 1 tbsp butter
- salt and pepper

You should only eat a little butter at a time.

Milk foods to eat for dinner

Many people like pasta and cheese. There are many kinds of pasta. There are also many kinds of cheeses. Find the two that you enjoy the most.

Every cheese has its own flavour.

Lemon yoghurt fruit dip

Please ask an adult to help you.

- Mix all the ingredients together in a bowl.
- Place in the refrigerator for 1–2 hours.
- Serve and enjoy with your favourite fruits.

You will need:
- 235 grams lemon yoghurt
- 235 grams crème fraîche
- 1 teaspoon (tsp) grated ginger
- 1 tablespoon honey
- ½ tsp lemon zest

Always try to buy low-**fat** yoghurt with little or no sugar. That is the healthiest.

Milk foods to eat for snacks

Frozen yoghurt is a great snack. It has less **fat** than ice cream, but is just as tasty. You can eat frozen yoghurt by itself, or with fruit toppings.

Use two different flavours of cheese to make your snack tastier.

For an easy snack, cut cheese into small cubes. Store the cheese in the refrigerator. When you want a fast snack, put some cubes into a bag and go.

Keeping milk foods fresh

Buy milk foods that are fresh. Always read the label on the food. Do not buy or drink milk after the **use-by date**. Do not drink milk that has turned **sour**.

Try and buy milk that will be fresh for at least a week.

Milk and most milk foods need to be stored in the refrigerator. Some cheeses can be kept outside the refrigerator. Be careful. Don't eat cheeses that have **mould** on the outside.

Do Milk Foods Alone Keep You Healthy?

Milk foods alone cannot keep you healthy. You need to eat many good foods. You should also drink three or four large glasses of water each day.

Exercise can be a lot of fun.

You need nine or more hours of sleep each night.

As well as eating healthy foods, your body needs regular **exercise**. You should try to do a little each day. You also need to get plenty of sleep each night. Sleep helps you stay strong and well.

Glossary

calcium mineral used to build and keep a person's bones and teeth strong

dairy place that prepares milk and milk foods, then sells them

diet what a person usually eats and drinks

exercise physical activity that helps keep a body healthy and fit

fat nutrient from food that gives you energy; a body only needs a little fat every day

food group foods that have the same kind of nutrients. There are five main food groups, plus oils.

graze feed on growing grasses

mild not sharp or strong in taste or odour

mineral nutrient needed to make the body work correctly

mould furry fungus that grows on old or spoiled food

nutrient substance (such as a vitamin or mineral) that the body needs to stay healthy and grow

protein nutrient in food that gives the body energy and helps it grow

sour sharp taste

tangy having a sharp or unusual flavour

use-by date date on food packaging that shows when it needs to be eaten by

vitamin nutrient in food that the body needs to stay healthy. Nutrients help the body work correctly.

Find out more

Books to read

Go Facts: Healthy Eating, Paul McEvoy (A & C Black, 2005)

Look After Yourself: Eat Healthy Food!, Angela Royston (Heinemann Library, 2004)

What's on Your Plate? Breakfast, Ted and Lola Schaefer (Raintree, 2006)

Websites to visit

www.5aday.nhs.uk
Click on "Fun & Games" and then "Did You Know?" to find out amazing food facts.

www.childrenfirst.nhs.uk/kids/health/eat_smart/food_science/index.html
Click on the milk and dairy products on the tray to find out more about why these are good for you and how many you need to eat each day.

www.nutrition.org.uk
Click on "Cook Club" for some great recipe ideas.

Index